MOVEMENT
IN
BLACK

Firebrand
Books
Ithaca, New York

This book may not be reproduced in whole or in part, except in the case
of reviews, without permission from Firebrand Books, 141 The Commons,
Ithaca, New York 14850.

Movement in Black was first published in 1978 by Diana Press and was
reissued in 1983 as part of the Crossing Press Feminist Series.

Book design by Wendy Cadden
Cover design by Betsy Bayley
Cover photograph by Marilyn Humphries
Illustrations by Wendy Cadden (frontispiece, 7, 41, 117), Irmagean (17,
    86, 88, 89, 90, 93), and Karen Sjoholm (95, 159)

Printed on acid-free paper in the United States by McNaughton & Gunn

Library of Congress Card No. 90-080060

Publisher's Note

Pat Parker—Black lesbian poet, feminist medical administrator, mother of two daughters, lover of women, softball devotee, and general progressive troublemaker—died of breast cancer on June 17, 1989 at the age of forty-five. I am pleased that Firebrand Books is able to publish this edition of her signature collection, *Movement In Black,* to coincide with Pat Parker's January 20th birthdate.

Originally produced in 1978 by Diana Press, *Movement In Black* went out of print several years later, a victim of the economically precarious condition of women's presses. It was reissued in 1983 as part of the Crossing Press Feminist Series. By 1987, *Movement In Black* was once again unavailable, a victim of changing priorities in alternative press publishing. It is appearing here in its third incarnation, part of a multi-genre, ethnically diverse feminist and lesbian publications list, alongside the author's companion volume of poetry, *Jonestown & Other Madness.*

Let us wish for *Movement In Black* that this book and its meanings thrive in the future, continuing to offer new generations of readers the vibrancy, vision, and strength of Pat Parker's voice.

Nancy K. Bereano
December 1989

CONTENTS

GRAPHICS BY
WENDY CADDEN
IRMAGEAN
KAREN SJOHOLM

Aya   The fern, a symbol of defiance

Nkyimkyim   Twisted pattern, meaning changing
one's self or playing many parts

Dedication

To my families
the one I was
born into
& the one I've chosen

FOREWORD

On the last night of my first trip to the West Coast in 1969, I walked into a room and met a young Black poet with fire in her eyes, a beer in her hand and a smile/scowl on her face. There were poems in her mouth, on the tables, in the refrigerator, under the bed, and in the way she cast about the apartment, searching for—not answers—but rather, unexpressable questions. We were both Black; we were Lesbians; we were both poets, in a very white, straight, male world, and we sat up all night trading poems. The next day the continent divided us, and during the next few years I read Pat Parker's two earlier books with appreciation, sometimes worrying about whether or not she'd/we'd survive. (Which for Black/Poet/Women is synonymous with grow).

Now, with love and admiration, I introduce Pat Parker and this new collection of her poetry. These poems would not need any introduction except for the racism and heterosexism of a poetry establishment which has whited out Parker from the recognition deserved by a dynamic and original voice in our poetry today.

> I am a child of America
> a step child
> raised in a back room

Even when a line falters, Parker's poetry maintains, reaches out and does not let go. It is clean and sharp without ever being neat. Yet her images are precise, and the plain accuracy of her visions encourages an honesty that may be uncomfortable as it is compelling. Her words are womanly and uncompromising.

SISTER! your foot's smaller
but it's still on my neck.

Her tenderness is very direct:

A woman's body must be taught to speak
bearing a lifetime of keys, a patient soul

and her directness can be equally tender:

My hands are big
and rough and callous
like my mother's-

Her Black Woman's voice rings true and deep and gentle, with an iron echo. It is merciless and vulnerable and far ranging. In her poems Parker owns her weaknesses and she owns her strengths, and she does not give up. Even when she weeps, her words evoke that real power which is core-born.

A pit is an abyss
let's drink to my shame

For as a Black Lesbian poet Parker knows, that for all women, the most enduring conflicts are far from simple.

And for the Sisters who still think that fear is a reason to be silent, Parker's poetry says loudly and clearly: I HAVE SURVIVED! I SEE, AND I SPEAK!

Audre Lorde

INTRODUCTION

The two graphic symbols (African) which designate the beginning of each poem and the dedication page of this collection were chosen by the author, Pat Parker. The one in front of poems is *Aya*, the fern, 'a symbol of defiance'. The second is *Nkyimkyim*, meaning 'changing one's self or playing many parts'.

After knowing Pat Parker for nearly ten years, I am not surprised by her choices, either for herself or for her work.

I asked her once about her personal idea of a revolution. What would she want to see happen. She said: "If I could take all my parts with me when I go somewhere, and not have to say to one of them, 'No, you stay home tonight, you won't be welcome,' because I'm going to an all-white party where I can be gay, but not Black. Or I'm going to a Black poetry reading, and half the poets are antihomosexual, or thousands of situations where something of what I am cannot come with me. The day all the different parts of me can come along, we would have what I would call a revolution." It is, as she says in one of her poems, a 'simple' dream.

Fortunately she has been a Goat Child, stubborn, persistent, ambitious, uncompromising, endowed with a powerful sense of justice-- and injustice. All the stuff she would need in order to shake poetry out of a kaleidoscope of overlapping oppressions. All the stuff she would need in order to get up and say what had never, before, anywhere, been said...about women, about lesbianism, about Blacks and whites living under a racist and sexist regime which strikes out from every side as well as from above...

Pat's first book, *Child of Myself*, appeared in 1972; her second is *Pit Stop*, 1973 and thirdly *Womanslaughter*, 1978 (Diana Press). In 1975 the two of us made a record together (Olivia Records). We called it in honor of ourselves as well as other women, 'Where Would I Be Without You.'

She is a magnificent reader, and I say that having heard her hundreds of times in wildly different situations--from rallies of 200,000 people to bars, conferences, churches, classrooms, TV studios.

To hear her is to take the various roles which compound her life--*to be them*. And because one of the parts which Parker plays is like a lawyer, it is in her poetry, the sensation of suddenly having a case formally presented to a court, and you will sometimes feel like the defendant, sometimes the jury or the judge.

Parker's way of working has always been to keep her ears open among a community of people, and take on the personal responsibility for saying what was on people's minds and important to them. What was not being said other places, or what was being muddied and needed clarification. And what white women could not hear at a meeting, we just might hear on a stage, boomed through a microphone. What men would not hold still for on the street, they might listen to in a more formal situation. Parker selects the work she reads for its effect on her audience, will it teach us anything--not, will it please us, will we like her, can she entertain us. This does not keep her from using sharply pointed sarcasm, irony, and a variety of hysterically funny senses to make her ideas come across.

I asked her what other poets had influenced her work. She handed me a small pile of paperbound books by poets, all of them Black, two thirds of them women. "And you," she said. I noticed that a number of the books were produced by independent Black presses, especially Dudley Randall's Broadside Press in Detroit, and the Third World Press from Chicago, extremely important sources of contemporary Black writing.

After reading them, I can see what she has learned from a poet like Don L. Lee, for instance--his bluntness and militancy, his spare language with the cutting edge out. Sonia Sanchez and Nikki Giovanni confirm. They all have that vital insistence on speaking a people's art, instead of an elite or academic art. I notice the warmth in the work and the philosophy of another woman writer, Lucille Clifton. Then on to Langston Hughes, contemporary as he can be, decade after decade. He published his first book in 1926. The last collection in 1969 shows me that he was much more blatant about struggling for the rights of Black people than was ever revealed by the selections of his work in the white English textbooks I recall from high school.

In addition to these people, I also know of Parker's admiration for Gwendolyn Brooks, Audre Lorde, Lorraine Hansberry, Zora Neale Hurston.

Obviously Pat Parker belongs to a continuing Black tradition of radical poetry. She has striven to keep her poetry close to its own origins and sources. Speaking in behalf of numberless other people, doing it in the first person.

As for original sources, she told me that she had modelled the form for her long poem *Womanslaughter* after my own marathon: *A Woman Is Talking to Death*. So I told her that *A Woman Is Talking to Death* was made the way it is because I was already so familiar with her own long autobiographical story-poem: *Goat Child*. What a Round Robin life is.

I remember laughing a particular way when I first heard *Goat Child* in 1970, and thought about it as a poem--the *presumption* of it. The feeling that she had truely *made something up*, something real, and yet so presumptuous. Like walking off the cliff and discovering you are flying. That sense that you or someone close to you has made something brand new, a new door opening. Which of course, opens the way for others (me) to go in that direction. She is an outrageous poet, the kind who says things first, and means them.

Goat Child was the first deliberately autobiographical poem by a woman that I had ever heard, although there was no reason (try sexism) why a woman's entire life couldn't be the storyline of a poem, a modern epic. For people hearing it at the time, the idea that women even *had* life stories was amazing and nearly unheard of. Parker was making literature out of stuff so buried under American racism and sexism, classism and antilesbianism that it wasn't even a question of breaking down or reversing a stereotype but of filling up a vacuum where the stereotype would have been if it were not *so* frightening for most people to even have such thoughts.

She has been one of the few poets to use sex between women as a subject. She calls them her X-rated poems, and found they have brought more censure than poems about overthrowing the government, bombs, etc. *Pit Stop* is the first poem I know of dealing with the subject of alcoholism among women, a serious debilitator of minority communities. *Womanslaughter*, which is much more than the chronicle of her sister's murder and her ex-brother-in-law's trial, and which she took to the International Tribunal on Crimes Against Women in Brussels, 1976, is a major work, a major American documentary poem and a feminist statement of commitment for women to defend other women from violent attack.

Daring to call herself a feminist from the beginning, when even other feminists had swallowed the false line that only white middleclass women need apply--what gall, for a movement which had half its own roots in the Black Power and Civil Rights struggles--Parker remained a feminist anyway-- lucky for the rest of us, giving direction, criticism, stamina, impetus, courage, and a spirit of resistance on stage and off.

Our lives are parallel in some ways. We are both from the Southwest. Parker grew up in the outskirts of Houston, one step away from the projects. She is one Texan who never brags about her state. We both had ugly tin roofs and no room to wave your arms, in a countryside vast with space. We were both miniature cowboys with boots and big imaginations. We both knew it was impossible for us to enter the world of poetry--and consequently we invented another world of poetry, and became peers, and leaders, and friends.

Above all it has mattered to me that she is a workingclass Black woman, drawing from Black art, Black political stances, Black cultural experience. Black historical remembrance.

I know that what we are doing with our work is the same; the experience will vary, but our basic work is the same, and the revolution which will gain us full status as human beings is the same revolution, and requires both of us. Pay attention. Parker has meant this to me, a focus on what is real, don't drift into a false...dream..an illusion of power...or safety... Pay attention to what matters.

She is actually a very traditional writer. Pat Parker continues the vital tradition of American Black literature, and along with Alta, Susan Griffin and myself, beginning in 1969 she revived a militant tradition of feminist writing on the West Coast. In addition she has helped found (or refound) a tremendously courageous line of poetry; the partially submerged tradition of lesbian poetry which dates from 600 BC.

Is this enough to say about her? No, because it doesn't say how much I love her as a person, or just how real the album cover title has been for me, as a sentence in my mind--Where would I be without you, Pat---*you*---Pat...

Judy Grahn

MARRIED

GOAT CHILD

I. 1944 - 1956

"you were a mistake"
my mother told me
ever since i've been
trying to make up.
couldn't really imagine
her/him in bed &
me coming 4 yrs after
the last sister
& to make things worse
i come blasting in
2 months too soon.
maybe the war did it
& to top the whole thing off
i'm the fourth girl
& was my father pissed.
caught pneumonia &
got hung up in incubator
for three months
finally made it out,
but the bed was too big
so my sister lost her doll bed.
another enemy quickly made.
& my old man being typical
spade businessman
too much credit - too little capital
loses his shop, &
we move to what is now
suburbs of Houston only
it had weeds and space

move to our own home
away from two-story brick
project where i found my
cousin's condom & blew it up
& good-bye cousins to
one room - tin roof playhouse
with tarzan making beams,
tin #2 washtub, maggot-filled
outhouse and super rats/
but i did try to please then.
football, baseball, fishing,
best yard cutter on the block.
two guns hanging from my hips
in the best Texas tradition
& me bad pistol pete holding
up all visitors for nickels
& wiping out roaches faster
than the durango kid ever could.
but even the best cowboys need learning
so they herded me back to school
but i remembered nursery school
& nurses with long needles
hell no i won't go,
but i went & had to leave
my guns/ could only take
my boots & the teacher
300 lbs. of don'ts
& i cried thru a whole day
of turtles, lizards, pretty
pictures, crayons, & glue.
came back all ready to
hang up the second day,

but the teacher showed
us her paddle - heavy
wood, hand fitted paddle
with holes drilled to
suck the flesh/ no tears
so i settled down &
fought my way thru first grade
defending my right to
wear cowboy boots even if
i was a girl which no one
had bothered to tell me
about at home / swung
into 2nd grade right into
economics/ 50¢ notebook
which mother couldn't
buy that day & i couldn't
tell the teacher that rap
so i copped one from the
doctor's son who could
afford it easy, but he
had numbered his pages
& i couldn't explain why
my book began on pg. 9
& the teacher calls
my sister who had been
her star #1 pupil
four years ago who
immediately denies that
her mother had bought it
& there i was a caught
thief at seven years old.
conditions improved/

looked like i was going
to make it till 5th grade
& i got beat all day
for stealing a 15¢ pack
of paper which i didn't,
but couldn't say because the
girl that did was too big
& the teacher got religion
& bought me steak sandwiches
from then on & even put me
in the glee club which was
indeed a most generous act.
& 6th grade was worse cause
oldest sister #2 had been
there & the teacher had
a good memory for bad ones.
& it wasn't until
i recited the night
before christmas
three times on our
class program that
she forgave me

II.

the goat left this child
me still trying to butt
my way in or out
& i came home dripping
blood & panic rode in
on my shoulders.
her slipped to the store

returned clutching a
box of kotex in a sack
twice as large.
"now you can have babies,
so keep your panties up"
& i couldn't see the
connection between me &
babies cause i wasn't
even thinking of marriage
& that always came first.
& him having to admit that
i really was a girl &
all of a sudden no more
football, not even touch
or anything & now getting
angry because i still
didn't like dolls &
all this time me not knowing
that the real hang up
was something called virginity
which i had already lost
2 years ago to a really
hard up rapist that i
never could tell my parents
about, not really knowing what
had happened but somehow
feeling it would not be
to my advantage.
twelve years old
& in southern baptists
tradition that meant
the leaving of childhood

& the latest acceptable
time to go to God
so with pleas of the
family image ringing
in my ears/ i went
baptism/ no evil spirit
left/ just cold & wet
waiting to be struck
down for fraud
& now mickey - a
baptism present to
replace delmonte
who replaced scotty
who replaced queen
who went mad and
ran thru the streets
foaming with me
climbing fences to
cut her off at the pass
but mickey a pup
already at my knees
orange, blue tongued
chow who ate on his
trainer who played with
his food and him brings
the victor to me/
scared but even more
afraid of it being
known & mickey just
as afraid as me, but
we learned and i
unchained him &

took the christmas
bike and rode free
miles and miles
& mickey running
ahead challenging
any one or dog to
get too close.
the goat came charging back
& my sisters could no
longer tell me
& the fights won in the day
lost when him came
at night, but renewed
each day with each new welt
& the boys at school
learned that him was crazy
& off to the jr. prom
with the faggot in the
church choir/ the only
acceptable male other
than him & the hate
chickens, ducks &
rabbits who ate their
young when i forgot
to put in more salt and
beatings and the volleyball
team i almost made varsity
but the gym floor & stitches
& better grades to apologize
pajama parties & mothers
who knew to go to bed
dirty jokes that i
didn't quite understand

& beer and drunkenness
the friend who always
imitated me clomping
the cha cha & never
saw my pain/ horns
shrank until senior
year & debate champion
who really wanted to
write but more afraid
of the coach who
knew i was the next
great spade lawyer
& failed the only
boy i ever loved to
make sure i didn't
get married/ her
pissed because i didn't get the
scholarship/ the big one
me who never told of
the little one that
would have kept me
in texas/ new pastures
for the goat.
   OUT
run to california
& golden streets
& big money
& freedom to go
anywhere & not being
served in new mexico
or arizona/ not stopping
to record that &
california streets

reeked of past glories
and wine and blood
and this brave young
goat blasting full
steam into everything
breaking the landlady's
window while showing
a young delinquent
a backhand & running
like hell; laughing
till it hurt &
his ole lady was
paying me to keep him out
of trouble
college and the german
who didn't want me
to know his language
& decided maybe adolph
wasn't so great after
all.
journalism
a friend who
cut her forearms
to commit suicide
& me offering to help
her do it right
& retired lady colonel
who didn't think i
liked her class &
this young beast
emphatically affirmed
her / journalism "C"

a little dark buddha
walked in with folder
"i'd like to see more
of your writing"/ me
awed - a man - who
knew about the goat.

III. 1962 - 1966

"I am a man,"
the buddha said-
come with me &
i will show you
the ways of woman.
come with me &
i will show you
the world of being -
the world of pain
the world of joy
the world of hate
the world of love
come walk with me
i will show you
why? - you are.
this goat-child charged
muscles tensed,
leaped, trampled
into a new time
a time of talk
a time of wine
parties & me
not knowing the words,

the gestures,
not knowing
history or heritage,
not knowing
the liars or their lies,
but sensing, somewhere
my head - hooded
allowed to breathe,
but not to see-
a blind goat charging
"I am a man,
the buddha said,
come with me &
i will show you
the ways of woman."
this goat saw & felt
the blood run,
leave my body-
i could not find the eyes,
no heart, no limbs
only blood, deep dark
blood that was life
that was dead -
scraped away
with a surgeon's knife.
scrapped into regret
scrapped into pain
non-existent,
but real,   real!
and the herds
herds of goats
herds of sheep
& the shepherds-

give me your milk
give me your wool
& we will feed you
we will protect you
the shepherds came
& taught me skills
to provide for them.
"come with me &
i will show you
the ways of woman"
& i learned
i learned hate
i learned jealousy
i learned my skills -
to cook - to fuck
to wash - to fuck
to iron - to fuck
to clean - to fuck
to care - to fuck
to wait - to fuck
& this goat-child cried
& screamed & ran
& the buddha's smile left
& his wisdom faded
& his throne crumbled
& the buddha left &
returned a shepherd.
in that leaving
the goat-child died-
the goat - child died
& a woman was born.

For Donna

Somewhere you live
and i
am many years   away,
no longer a frighten child
capable only of giving birth.

i wonder of your mother

not me -

>   for i have never washed you
>   never fed you
>   never touched you.

If she tells you of me,
>   will you understand?

understand my choice =

>   give away a part of myself
>   to save a part of myself

If she tells you of me,

>   will you hate me?

>   i know hate.
>   i know the hate of your father,
>   i know the hate of the mothers -
>   who kept their children,

i will accept your hate

but my child,

>   you can never hate me

as much as I have hated myself.

Sometimes my husband
acts
just like a man...

dishes are evil / you know
they can destroy the spirit...

Washing dishes should
be outlawed

paper plate nirvana!

long live dixie cups!

...tomorrow i am going to lose
my temper -

i will destroy all the dishes
that i missed last week -

Fuller Brush Day

Here you are, lady,
a year's supply of room spray,
& I watch myself
walking down
my hall,
spraying for a year.
Spraying for a year,
spray here - spray there
walking down my hall
spraying room spray,
An artificial forest
wiping out city smells.
Artificial forest,
minus birds
minus squirrels,
minus dew
minus--
spraying for a year.

If you run out before
a year's time
we'll give you another bottle
Another bottle
a full
definite
permanent year's bottle

permanent year
365 ¼ days
no time given
to holidays
one year,
spray for a year
phony forest
for a year
forest in my kitchen
forest in my toilet
forest in my cat box
a full time-
real life forest
smelling type year.
walking down my halls
spraying for a year
365 ¼ days
of spray
spray
spray
& I bought it.

To see a man cry -
is like watching animals
in a zoo,
  say
the baby elephant
      whose trunk is
          too short
          or my arm
isn't long enough
and the peanuts
won't quite reach
          but fall among husks
like your tears
          mating with mine
  in frustration

Even in our worst times
some part of us -
finds each other.

You can't be sure of anything these days.

    you meet a really far out man -
    tells you,
    he's been on his own for years
       opens car doors for you
       carries packages for you
       protects you from evil doers
Says he wants an intelligent, creative
    woman to be his *partner* in life.

          you marry and find
the dude is
       too weak to pick up a dish
       too dumb to turn on a burner
       too afraid to do laundry
       too tense to iron a shirt
& to top the whole thing off -
he tries to cover his incompetence,
by telling YOU -
       it's women's work.

You can't be sure of anything these days.

"a going out or going forth;
departure."

Exodus (To my husbands, lovers)

Trust me no more -
Our bed is unsafe.
Hidden within folds of cloth
a cancerous rage -

i will serve you no more
in the name of wifely love
i'll not masturbate your pride
in the name of wifely loyalty

Trust me no more
Our bed is unsafe
Hidden within folds of cloth
    a desperate slave

You dare to dismiss my anger
    call it woman's logic
You dare to claim my body
    call it wifely duty

Trust me no more
Your bed is unsafe
    Rising from folds of cloth -

A Moment Left Behind

Have you ever tried to catch a tear?
Catch it on bent fingers.
Press it against your eyelids,
And wish the moment gone.

Or capture bitter words
Ripped from your throat like timber
And surround them -
islands of instants.

I do not claim all possible
Creating myths of modern America.
I cannot swim an ocean.
I attempt the width of a pool.

From Deep Within

Nature tests those she would call hers;
Slips us, naked and blank down dark paths.
Skeletons of the sea, this we would become
to suck a ray of sight from the fire.

A woman's body must be taught to speak-
Bearing a lifetime of keys, a patient soul,
moves through a maze of fear and bolts
clothed in soft hues and many candles.

The seasons' tongues must be heard & taken,
And many paths built for the travelers.
A woman's flesh learns slow by fire and pestle,
Like succulent meats, it must be sucked and eaten.

LIBERATION FRONTS

My hands are big
   and rough & callused -
   like my mother's

My innards are twisted
   and torn and sectioned -
   like my father's

Now - some of
   my sisters see me
   as big & twisted
     rough & torn
     callused & sectioned
   definitely not pleasant,
   to be around -

          I
Had i listened to my father

i would be
married & miserable
   dreaming of fish
   & open space
   & bellowing my needs -
     waiting for some one
     to listen to the second run
     & know -

it is difficult to be
   strong -
   & appear sure
no one ever believes
   when you cry

II

Had i listened to my mother
i would be married & miserable
   dreaming - praying
   of security
& choking on my needs
   waiting for some one
   to listen to the second run
   & know

It is difficult to be
   quiet -
   & appear sure
no one believes
   when you
      don't
   show your tears.

III

My hands are big & rough
   like my mother's
my innards are twisted & torn
   like my father's
my self is
   my big hands -
      like my father's
   & torn innards
      like my mother's
   & they both felt
      & were -
& i am a product of that -
& not a political consciousness

"This at last is bone of my bones
and flesh of my flesh;
she shall be called Woman,
because she was taken out of
Man."

Genesis I: 23

from cavities of bones
spun
from caverns of air
i, woman - bred of man
taken from the womb of sleep;
i, woman that comes
before the first.

to think second
to believe first
a mistake
erased by the motion of years.
i, woman, i
can no longer claim
a mother of flesh
a father of marrow
I, Woman must be
the child of myself.

"There are two things I've got a
right to, and these are death
or liberty. One or the other
i mean to have."

Harriet Tubman

Brother
   I don't want to hear
   about
   how *my* real enemy
   is the system.
i'm no genius,
   but i do know
   that system
you hit me with
   is called
   a fist.

"How do we know that the panthers
will accept a gift from
white - middle - class - women?"

Have you ever tried to hide?

   In a group

          of women

                 hide

       yourself

slide between the floor boards

slide yourself away child

   away from this room

     & your sister

before she notices

    your Black self &

her white mind

          slide your eyes

         down

away from the other Blacks

   afraid - a meeting of eyes

& pain would travel between you -

    change like milk to buttermilk

    a silent rage.

       SISTER!   your foot's smaller,

but it's still on my neck.

In English Lit.,
  they told me
Kafka was good
  because he created
the best nightmares ever-
I think I should
go find that professor
& ask why
we didn't study
the S.F. Police Dept.

My heart is fresh cement,
Still able to mark on,
but in short time,
No,
    I will not dry,
      covering streets of men
           with hate.

BLOW HOT SOUL SISTER,
    My breath leaves me -
arid words crack,
        tumble, to the floor
like spilled salt.

Hate - Kill - hate - kill

That's primitive -

Yes, primitive,

    Be

Run naked thru jungles,

    run

      run,

wallow in trampled grass,

    trampled,

      run,

be, primitive

                 like sex -

filthy,

           sweaty,   be

hate,

         my guts ache

KEEP   your guns,

         or you die first   run

kill, hate, run,

               killhaterundie

primitive/free

         hate   kill
NO!

      wet grass is sticky.

Dialogue

Mother, dear mother, I'm dying,
People are frowning at me,
I spend my time now, crying,
I don't know what to be.

Child, dear child, I'm sad,
To know you've gone astray,
Beatniks, you know, are bad,
I hope you find the way.

Mother, dear mother, I'm frightened,
They're dropping bombs about my head,
I'm afraid to bother to make a friend,
For I'm sure she'd wind up dead.

Child, dear child, you're silly,
The bombs are for the enemy,
And every good person is willing,
To help keep our country free.

Mother, dear mother, I'm passed,
Working my whole life away,
Trying to join a higher class,
& living in utter decay.

* Child, dear child, I must,
Show you the way to God,
First, you learn to trust,
& stop doing things that are odd.

*by Shirley Jones

Mother, dear mother, are you blind?
You've seen nothing I've said,
What will you do when you find,
Your child has fallen down dead?

Child, dear child, I'll buy,
A large casket made of gold,
I'll sit beside you and cry,
& pray to God for your soul.

With the sun -

fear leaves me

rushes to cover/

leaves lumps

like the backyard gopher

to remind me.

I am afraid

of anyone

of anything

that would harm me/

not the pain

not the act

but,

    the desire.

"What are you, Michael?"
"Black and Beautiful."

For Michael on his third birthday.

A distant time passed
Men chained back to back
Destined pain by cast
Slave - night men - Black

Overseers of then & tomorrow
Families born into a pack
Believing - that they borrow
Slaves - dead men - Black

Hurt - doubters of the lie
Death the only fact
Teach the son to die
Slaves - free men - Black

Slaves, dead, under ground
Fire swallows the rack
The gun has turned around
MEN - Beautiful and Black

"Cursed be Canaan;
a slave of slaves
shall he be to his
brothers."

Genesis 9: 25

A FAMILY TREE

Pitch sun-child drowns in the Mississippi,
washes away chains of loneliness, floats
a drum beat on the Nile.

Daughter of Ham lies on a church floor;
filled in orgasm with her Maker,
a spent lover ignorant of a hard bed.

The sperm of a million nights
sings loud over the southern skies;
- Sirens to a nation's conscience.

A babe of illusion has been born.
She will tell the world of rainbows;
And kiss the holes in its eyes.

Sunday

Each Sunday
   the people   of this town
would go to church
   eat dinner
     all at one table with their family
   the television silent
    & bless the food,
      father
        we thank
         THEE
   & their maids
off
     with their families
   & everyone rest
   until the Sunday
    when the rains
    began
      and crashed
      thru the wind
    moving away the dirt
    but somebody didn't
    stop it
     and the
  little river
    rose
       and
         rose
   till the cars
   and televisions
   and blankets

and people - all
washed thru the
    streets and past
    their neighbors'
    for blocks
    and blocks

The troops came on Wednesday
The water had
    stopped
    the wet
merged with the dirt
    mud
            was
    all over
        and
    the troops shook their heads.

They could not
        bury
        the dead.

    In the
        death murk

they couldn't tell
        the
        Black
        from
        the white.

Pied Piper

She sits,
ebony skinned,
drawing sun rays.
Children cluster;
a jagged circle
presses inward.
Sand - covered feet
Lean,
in homage to
the High Priestess.
The classical reed
will not suffice.

A Conga

Willowy notes
are not heard.
Deep, tense, beats
climb down the drum,
Jumping out in the air,
Lions roaring at children.

Conga

Black hands
beat the skin;
a white bred
with sweat.

Conga

Drum beats
dance over the waves,
& children's kyaks
drift inward.

The priestess rests.
Her fingers cuddle
the drum head.
Children query, with
eyes showing no hate.
"What kinda drum is it?"
"Conga"
"You play good;
Is it a message?"
"Message?"
"Yes, does it mean?
What song is it?"

"It's a Mau Mau death song."

i wonder
how many matches
it would take,
to lay a single-file trail
from here -
to richard nixon's ass.

It's probably not a good idea.
I can see him now -
Waving his singed prick
on nation-wide television,
telling how it was saved
by a tub of confidence
provided by
his silent majority.

Where do you go to become a non-citizen?

I want to resign; I want out.
I want to march to the nearest place
Give my letter to a smiling face
I want to resign; I want out.

President Ford vetoed a jobs bill
Sent to him from capital hill
While we sit by being super cool
He gets a $60,000 swimming pool
I wanna resign; I want out.

$68,000 to Queen Elizabeth to not grow cotton.
Yet there's no uproar that this jive is rotten.
$14,000 to Ford Motors to not plant wheat
I guess the government don't want wheat all over the seats.
I wanna resign; I want out.

The CIA Commission was in session for 26 weeks long
Said the boys didn't do too much wrong
They gave out acid- a test- so they tell
Yet, if you and I used it- we'd be in jail.
I wanna resign; I want out.

And from Taft College- a small group of fools
Chased all the Black students out of the school.
And good citizens worried about property sale
Chased away Black teenagers from picturesque Carmel.
I wanna resign; I want out.

The little league after using all excuses up
Says a 10 year old girl must use a boys supportive cup
An international Women's Congress in Mexico to make plans
Elected for their president - a white-liberal man.
I wanna resign; I want out.

The A.P.A. finally said all gays aren't ill
Yet ain't no refunds on their psychiatry bills.
A federal judge says MCC is valid - a reality
Yet it won't keep the pigs from hurting you or me
I wanna resign; I want out.

I wanna resign; I want out.
Please lead me to the place
Show me the smiling face
I'm skeptical-full of doubt
I wanna resign; I want out.

"Don't let the fascist speak."
"We want to hear what they have to say."
"Keep them out of the classroom."
"Everybody is entitled to freedom of speech."

I am a child of America
a step child
      raised in the back room
yet taught
      taught how to act
in her front room.
my mind jumps
the voices of students
screaming
insults   threats
"Let the Nazis speak"
"Let the Nazis speak"
Everyone is entitled
      to speak
I sit a greasy-legged
      Black child
in a Black school
in the Black part of town
look to a Black teacher
the bill of rights
      guarantees
us all the right
      my mind
remembers   chants
article I   article I
& my innards churn
they remember

the Black teacher
in the Black school
in the Black part
of the very white town
who stopped us
when we attacked
the puppet principal
the white Board
of mis-Education
cast-off books
illustrated with
cartoons and
words of wisdom
written by white
children in the
other part of town
missing pages
caricatures
of hanging niggers —
the bill of rights
was written to
> *protect*
>> *us*

my mind remembers
& my innards churn
conjure images
> police
break up
illegal demonstrations
illegal assemblies
> conjure image
of a Black Panther

"if tricky Dick
tries to stop us
we'll stop him."
        conjure image
of that same Black man
going to jail
for threatening
the life of
        THE PRESIDENT
every citizen
is entitled to
freedom of speech
my mind remembers
& my innards churn
conjure images
of jews in camps —
of homosexuals in camps —
of socialists in camps —
"Let the Nazis speak"
"Let the Nazis speak"
        faces in a college
        classroom
"You're being fascist too."
"We want to hear what
they have to say"

        faces in
a college classroom
young white faces
        speak let them speak
speak let them speak
Blacks jews some whites
seize the bull horn

"We don't want to hear
your socialist rhetoric"
    socialist rhetoric
    survival
           rhetoric
the supreme court
says it is illegal
to scream fire
in a crowded theatre

to scream fire
in a crowded theatre
cause people to panic
to run to hurt each other
my mind remembers
& now i know
what my innards
     say
illegal to cause
     people
to panic
to run
to hurt
there is
no contradiction
what the Nazis say
will cause
     people
     to hurt
     ME.

To My Vegetarian Friend

It's not called soul food
because it goes with music.
It is a survival food

    from the grease
sprang generations
of my people
      generations
of slaves
that ate the leavings
  of their masters
    & survived

And when I sit —
faced by
chitterlins & greens
neckbones & tails
it is a ritual —
it is a joining —
me to my ancestors
& your words ring untrue
this food is good for me
It replenishes my soul

so if you really
can't stand
to look at my food
can't stand
to smell my food
& can't keep those feelings
    to yourself

Do us both a favor
    & stay home

For the white person who wants to know
how to be my friend.

The first thing you do is to forget that i'm Black.
Second, you must never forget that i'm Black.

You should be able to dig Aretha,
but don't play her every time i come over.
And if you decide to play Beethoven — don't tell me
his life story. They made us take music appreciation too.

Eat soul food if you like it, but don't expect me
to locate your restaurants
or cook it for you.

And if some Black person insults you,
mugs you, rapes your sister, rapes you,
rips your house or is just being an ass —
please, do not apologize to me
for wanting to do them bodily harm.
It makes me wonder if you're foolish.

And even if you really believe Blacks are better lovers than
whites — don't tell me. I start thinking of charging stud fees.

In other words — if you really want to be my friend — *don't*
make a labor of it. I'm lazy. Remember.

Tour America!
a T.V. commercial said.
I will -
there are things I need:
    travelers checks in new york
    gas mask in berkeley,
    face mask in los angeles,
National guardsmen to protect me
    - in the south,
Marines to protect me
    from guardsmen
    - in the mid-west,
Police to protect me
    from hustlers
    - in the ghettos,
Bullet-proof vest and helmet
    to protect me from police
    - everywhere

Tour America!
perhaps,
    it would be better

to blow it up.

I'm so tired
of hearing about
  capitalist
  sexist,
  racist,
  fascist
  chauvinist,
  feminist.

I am tired
of hearing about
  confrontating
  demonstrating
  trashing,
  smashing,
  surviving,
  jiving.

I'm beginning to
wonder if
the tactics
of this revolution
  is to
talk the enemy to death.

The *What* Liberation Front?

Today i had a talk with my dog
he called me a racist - chauvinist person.
told me he didn't like the way
i keep trying to change him.
Dogs - he said - do not shit in toilets
Dogs - like to shit out side & he didn't
appreciate being told to shit in the gutter -
just because i didn't like the smell of his shit -
he informed me that fish weren't so hot
about my shit either.
And property - he wanted to know why
people expected dogs to protect their capitalist interest
he never watches television or plays
records. & how come i put tags on him.
My dog - he laughed. He is his own dog.
And what's this bullshit about his sex
life. If he wants to fuck in the streets it's
his business & the genocide against dogs -
Now by this time he's growling - & i just
said - he didn't have to get nasty - i was
willing to study the problem. After all didn't
i buy him good bones and get him groomed
once a month & then he starts hollering
about if he wanted to get dirty &
have long hair that was his right too.
And another thing he said - if he wants to
sit he'll sit - so just shovel my shit about
sit, lie, roll over, stand up. And finally
he said standing up - the next time i patted
him on the head & called him a good boy
he was gonna lift his leg - With that,
he got up & left the house saying something
about a consciousness-raising meeting.

Snatches of a Day

Grey clouds floated past my window -

    & I ignored them,
    danced into the streets,
    stoned on life.

A woman with brown hair

    like dirty corduroy,
    riding in a Malibu,
    with an olive green suit,
    & a big cigar
    stared at me.
I stopped dancing.

An old cripple dragged past me -

    I offered to carry her;
    She called me a nigger.
      I cut her throat,
      danced around her head,
      sang, "We Shall Overcome."
      hung her scalp over Woolworth's candy counter.

Cops started to arrest me.
    Said I couldn't dance without a permit.
    So, I skipped slowly.

Science teacher lectured for an hour,
    Never did tell me his name,
    So, I didn't tell him mine,
Just my student body & social security numbers.

A friend gave me a God's eye -
    Shocked me,
    Didn't know He had eyes.

My cousin died last week
    He was a hero.
    Died defending my liberty -
    O sweet liberty
    Land of the free
    & the great.

Went to a dull movie.
Watched a guy masturbate.

I want to go to sleep.
My cat won't let me under the covers.

Boots are being polished
Trumpeters clean their horns
Chains and locks forged
The crusade has begun.

Once again flags of Christ
are unfurled in the dawn
and cries of soul saviors
sing apocalyptic on air waves.

Citizens, good citizens all
parade into voting booths
and in self-righteous sanctity
X away our right to life.

I do not believe as some
that the vote is an end,
I fear even more
It is just a beginning.

So I must make assessment
Look to you and ask:
Where will you be
when they come?

They will not come
a mob rolling
through the streets,
but quickly and quietly
move into our homes
and remove the evil,

the queerness,
the faggotry,
the perverseness
from their midst.
They will not come
clothed in brown,
and swastikas, or
bearing chest heavy with
gleaming crosses.
The time and need
for ruses are over.
They will come
in business suits
to buy your homes
and bring bodies to
fill your jobs.
They will come in robes
to rehabilitate
and white coats
to subjugate
and where will you be
when they come?

Where will we *all be*
when they come?
And they will come-

they will come
because we are
defined as opposite-
perverse
and we are perverse.

Every time we watched
a queer hassled in the
streets and said nothing-
It was an act of perversion.

Everytime we lied about
the boyfriend or girlfriend
at coffee break -
It was an act of perversion.

Everytime we heard,
"I don't mind gays
but why must they
be blatant?" and said nothing-
It was an act of perversion.

Everytime we let a lesbian mother
lose her child and did not fill
the courtrooms-
It was an act of perversion.

Everytime we let straights
make out in our bars while
we couldn't touch because
of laws-
It was an act of perversion.

Everytime we put on the proper
clothes to go to a family
wedding and left our lovers
at home-
It was an act of perversion.

Everytime we heard
"Who I go to bed with
is my personal choice-
It's personal not political"
and said nothing-
It was an act of perversion.

Everytime we let straight relatives
bury our dead and push our
lovers away-
It was an act of perversion.

And they will come.
They will come for
the perverts

& it won't matter
if you're
      homosexual, not a faggot
      lesbian, not a dyke
      gay, not queer
It won't matter
if you
      own your business
      have a good job
      or are on S.S.I.
It won't matter
if you're
      Black
      Chicano
      Native American
      Asian
      or White

It won't matter
if you're from
    New York
    or Los Angeles
    Galveston
    or Sioux Falls
It won't matter
if you're
    Butch, or Fem
    Not into roles
    Monogamous
    Non Monogamous
It won't matter
If you're
    Catholic
    Baptist
    Atheist
    Jewish
    or M.C.C.

They will come
They will come
to the cities
and to the land
to your front rooms
and in *your* closets.

They will come for
the perverts
and where will
you be
When they come?

"Until all oppressed people
are free -
none of us are free."

Questions

I

the chains are different now -
lay on this body strange
no metal clanging in my ears

chains laying strange
chains laying light-weight
laying credit cards
laying welfare forms
laying buying on time
laying white packets of dope
laying afro's & straighten hair
laying pimp & revolutionary
laying mother & daughter
laying father & son

chains laying strange -
strange laying chains
        chains

how do i break these chains

II

the chains are different now -
laying on this body strange
funny chains - no clang -

chains laying strange
chains laying light-weight
chains laying dishes
chains laying laundry
chains laying grocery markets
chains laying no voice
chains laying children
chains laying *selective* jobs
chains laying less pay
chains laying girls & women
chains laying wives & women
chains laying mothers & daughters

chains laying strange
strange laying chains
    chains

how do i break these chains

III

the chains are still here
laying on this body strange
no metal - no clang
chains laying strange
chains laying light-weight
chains laying funny
chains laying different
chains laying dyke
chains laying bull-dagger
chains laying pervert
chains laying no jobs
chains laying more taxes

chains laying beatings
chains laying stares
chains laying myths
chains laying fear
chains laying revulsion

chains laying strange
strange laying chains
    chains

how do i break these chains

IV

the chains are here
no metal - no clang
chains of ignorance & fear
chains here - causing pain

how do i break these chains
to whom or what
    do i direct pain
    Black - white
    mother - father
    sister - brother
    straight - gay

how do i break these chains
how do i stop the pain
who do i ask - to see
what must i do - to be free

sisters - how do i break your chains
brothers - how do i break your chains

mothers - how do i break your chains
fathers - how do i break your chains

    i don't want to kill -
    i don't want to cause pain -

how -
how else do i break - your chains.

i have a dream
  no -
  not Martin's
though my feet moved
  down many paths.
  it's a simple dream -

i have a dream
  not the dream of the vanguard
  not to turn this world -
    all over
  not the dream of the masses -
    not the dream of women
    not to turn this world
      all
          over
it's a simple dream -

In my dream -
  i can walk the streets
    holding hands with my lover

In my dream -
  i can go to a hamburger stand
    & not be taunted by bikers on a holiday.

In my dream -
  i can go to a public bathroom,
    & not be shrieked at by ladies -

In my dream -
  i can walk ghetto streets
    & not be beaten up by my brothers.

In my dream -
   i can walk out of a bar
   & not be arrested by the pigs

I've placed this body
   placed this mind
   in lots of dreams -
   in Martin's & Malcolm's -
   in Huey's & Mao's -
   in George's & Angela's -
   in the north & south
      of Vietnam & America
      & Africa

i've placed this body & mind
   in dreams -
   dreams of people -

now i'm tired -
now you listen!
   i have a dream too.
   it's a simple dream.

MOVEMENT IN BLACK

Movement in Black
movement in Black
can't keep em back
movement in Black

I
They came in ships
from a distant land
bought in chains
to serve the man

I am the slave
that chose to die
I jumped overboard
& no one cried

I am the slave
sold as stock
walked to and fro
on the auction block

They can be taught
if you show them how
they're strong as bulls
and smarter than cows.

I worked in the kitchen
cooked ham and grits
seasoned all dishes
with a teaspoon of spit.

I worked in the fields
picked plenty of cotton
prayed every night
for the crop to be rotten.

All slaves weren't treacherous
that's a fact that's true
but those who were
were more than a few.

Movement in Black
Movement in Black
Can't keep em back
Movement in Black

II

I am the Black woman
& i have been all over
when the colonists
fought the British
i was there
i aided the colonist
i aided the British
i carried notes,
stole secrets,
guided the men
& nobody thought
to bother me
i was just a
Black woman
the britishers lost
and I lost,
but I was there
& i kept on moving

I am the Black woman
& i have been all over
i went out west, yeah
the Black soldiers
had women too,
& i settled the land,
& raised crops & children,
but that wasn't all

i hauled freight,
& carried mail,
drank plenty whiskey
shot a few men too.
books don't say much
about what I did
but I was there
& i kept on moving.

I am the Black woman
& i have been all over
up on platforms & stages
talking about freedom
freedom for Black folks
freedom for women
In the civil war too
carrying messages,
bandaging bodies
spying and lying
the south lost
& i still lost
but i was there
& i kept on moving

I am the Black woman
& I have been all over
I was on the bus
with Rosa Parks
& in the streets
with Martin King

I was marching
and singing
and crying
and praying
I was with SNCC
& i was with CORE
I was in Watts
when the streets
were burning
I was a panther
in Oakland
In new york
with N.O.W.
In San Francisco
with gay liberation
in D.C. with
the radical dykes
yes, I was there
& i'm still moving

movement in Black
movement in Black
can't keep em back
movement in Black

III
I am the Black woman

I am Bessie Smith
singing the blues
& all the Bessies
that never sang a note

I'm the southerner
who went north
I'm the northener
who went down home

I'm the teacher
in the all Black school
I'm the graduate
who cannot read

I'm the social worker
in the city ghetto
I'm the car hop
in a delta town

I'm the junkie with a jones
I'm the dyke in the bar
I'm the matron at county jail
I'm the defendant with nothin' to say.

I'm the woman with 8 kids
I'm the woman who didn't have any
I'm the woman who poor as sin
I'm the woman who's got plenty.

I'm the woman who
raised white babies &
taught my kids to
raise themselves.

movement in Black
movement in Black
can't keep em back
movement in Black

IV
Roll call, shout em out

Phyliss Wheatley
Sojourner Truth
Harriet Tubman
Frances Ellen Watkins Harper
Stagecoach Mary
Lucy Prince
Mary Pleasant
Mary McLeod Bethune
Rosa Parks
Coretta King
Fannie Lou Hammer
Marion Anderson
& Billies
& Bessie
sweet Dinah
A-re-tha
Natalie
Shirley Chisolm
Barbara Jordan
Patricia Harris
Angela Davis
Flo Kennedy
Zora Neale Hurston
Nikki Giovanni
June Jordan
Audre Lorde
Edmonia Lewis
and me
and me
and me
and me
and me

& all the names we forgot to say
& all the names we didn't know
& all the names we don't know, yet.

movement in Black
movement in Black
Can't keep em back
movement in Black

V

I am the Black woman
I am the child of the sun
the daughter of dark
I carry fire to burn the world
I am water to quench its throat
I am the product of slaves
I am the offspring of queens
I am still as silence
I flow as the stream

I am the Black woman
I am a survivor
I am a survivor
I am a survivor
I am a survivor
I am a survivor

Movement in Black.

This poem was first performed at Oakland
Auditorium on December 2nd and 3rd 1977
by Linda Tillery, Vicki Randle, Alberta
Jackson, Mary Watkins and Pat Parker

BEING GAY

Move in darkness
know the touch of a woman

a wall of normalcy
wraps your body -
strangles
brightens

wrinkled ugliness

sin

fear

admission

Two days later

you shudder

& take 2 aspirins

1

My lover is a woman
   & when i hold her -
     feel her warmth -
     i feel good - feel safe

then/ i never think of
   my families' voices -
   never hear my sisters say -
   bulldaggers, queers, funny -
   come see us, but don't
   bring your friends -
   it's okay with us,
   but don't tell mama
     it'd break her heart
   never feel my father
   turn in his grave
   never hear my mother cry
   Lord, what kind of child is this?

2

My lover's hair is blonde
   & when it rubs across my face
     it feels soft -
   feels like a thousand fingers
   touch my skin & hold me
   and i feel good.

then/ i never think of the little boy
   who spat & called me nigger
   never think of the policemen
   who kicked my body and said crawl

never think of Black bodies
hanging in trees or filled
with bullet holes
never hear my sisters say
white folks hair stinks
don't trust any of them
never feel my father
turn in his grave
never hear my mother talk
of her back ache after scrubbing floors
never hear her cry -
Lord, what kind of child is this?

3

My lover's eyes are blue
& when she looks at me
i float in a warm lake
    feel my muscles go weak with want
        feel good - feel safe

Then/ i never think of the blue
    eyes that have glared at me -
    moved three stools away from me
        in a bar
    never hear my sisters rage
    of syphilitic Black men as
        guinea pigs -
    rage of sterilized children -
    watch them just stop in an
    intersection to scare *the old
        white bitch.*
    never feel my father turn
        in his grave

never remember my mother
teaching me the yes sirs & mams
    to keep me alive -
never hear my mother cry,
Lord, what kind of child is this?

4

And when we go to a gay bar
    & my people shun me because i crossed
        the line
    & her people look to see what's
    wrong with her - what defect
    drove her to me -

And when we walk the streets
    of this city - forget and touch
    or hold hands and the people
    stare, glare, frown, & taunt
    at those queers -

I remember-
    Every word taught me
    Every word said to me
    Every deed done to me
    & then i hate -
    i look at my lover
    & for an instance - doubt -

Then/ i hold her hand tighter
And i can hear my mother cry.
Lord, what kind of child is this.

"i like your friends.
they're real people.
not phony - like your
sisters' friends."

Marie Cooks

COP - OUT

To My Mother

All of these
real people -
are real,
   live in the
    flesh
     dykes -
& all the boyfriends
   that they have
   are a part of my creativity.

All of these real people
   are real -
& i can only tell you
   real live in the flesh -
     lies -

For Willyce

When i make love to you
   i try
      with each stroke of my tongue
         to say   i love you
         to tease i love you
         to hammer   i love you
         to melt   i love you

     & your sounds drift down
       oh god!
         oh jesus!
      and i think -
here it is, some dude's
getting credit for what
    a woman
     has done,
        again.

Best Friends
(for Whitey)

So how come
we can't touch
when we hurt most?
    Can only
    sense &
    hurl ourselves
against forces
& each other
& laugh away
our agony
        tomorrow -
as drunk
yesterdays.

Pit Stop

A pit is a covered hole
used to trap wild animals.

a pit is an abyss.

a pit is the ground floor
of a theatre,
    especially the part
at the rear.

a pit is a coward's suicide.

a hearty drink to anything -

Let us drink to your new lover
Let us drink to your lover - gone
Let us drink to my lover
Let us drink to my lover - gone
Hey let's drink to the good people
Let's drink to the nearest holiday

Let's drink to our ability to drink.

A pit is a covered hole

used by wild animals

it's hard to withdraw the fangs, now

in public places

the anger spills over

to be mopped away, later

too much drink

slow fang withdrawal

our animalism is showing

a bad image -

Let's drink to a bad image

Let's drink to a covered pit

  & happy animals

& withdrawn fangs

a pit is an abyss

Let's drink to my shame.

  a hustle

a grand hustle

i love you, so

i won't call you fool.

Let's have another drink

you love me

you won't walk away from me.

Let's have another drink

    to our hustle

let's hustle another drink

    & drink

to our ability to hustle.

Let's have a drink to our shame.

Let's have a drink

    to drink

a pit is the ground floor

of a theatre,

especially the part

at the rear.

It was a good show last night

full of venom

i thought for sure she would hit her

& did you see that woman fall off her stool?

yes indeed a grand show

everybody was

& it ended safely -

How's your head this morning dearie?

Let's drink to a good show

Let's drink to the rear of the theatre.

It's hard to get hit with a bottle here.

Just watch the show.

Let's drink to a ground floor.

Has anyone ever priced the
                    balcony?

a pit is a coward's suicide.

what do you mean kill yourself.

that's a bummer - makes me sad.

Let's have another drink.

yes, i've gained weight -
it's the beer you know.

cold - yes
caught a lot of colds -

just need to take more vitamin C

Let's have a hot toddie for my cold.

wow that's too bad - over dose huh.

won't touch the stuff -

if anything kills me
it will be the booze, ha ha.

Let's have a drink to her & her drug.

she was a good kid

One of these days i'll have a check-up -

getting winded too easily - getting old.

Let's have another drink.

i can't imagine anyone committing suicide.

the mechanics are too slow here.

the tires should be on -
   the gas in.

what's the matter?

you want to cost us the race?

Oh - one more drink

Let's drink to the race.
Let's drink to the pit crew.
Let's drink,
            let's drink
let us drink
            let us drink
                    drink
                    drink

excuse me friends,
            i must go now

i cannot afford to lose
            this race.

i cannot afford to die,
            in this place

"Give strong drink unto him
  that is ready to perish, and
  wine unto those that be of
  heavy hearts. Let him drink
  and forget his poverty, and
  remember his misery no more."
                    Proverbs 31 :6-7

When i drink
    i scream
    i fight
    i cry

    i don't
      do these things

      when i'm sober.

so far,

my friends

think the
solution

to my being

a problem

is for me
to stop

drinking.

For The Straight Folks
Who Don't Mind Gays
But Wish They Weren't So BLATANT

you know some people
got a lot of nerve.
sometimes, i don't believe
the things i see and hear.

Have you met the woman
who's shocked by 2 women kissing
& in the same breath,
tells you that she's pregnant?
BUT GAYS SHOULDN'T BE BLATANT.

Or this straight couple
sits next to you in a movie
& you can't hear the dialogue
Cause of the sound effects.
BUT GAYS SHOULDN'T BE BLATANT.

And the woman in your office
Spends your entire lunch hour
talking about her new bikini drawers
& how much her husband likes them.
BUT GAYS SHOULDN'T BE BLATANT.

Or the "hip" chick in your class,
rattling a mile a minute —
while you're trying to get stoned
in the john
about the camping trip she took
with her musician boyfriend.
BUT GAYS SHOULDN'T BE BLATANT.

You go in a public bathroom
And all over the walls
there's John loves Mary,
Janice digs Richard,
Pepe loves Delores, etc. etc.
BUT GAYS SHOULDN'T BE BLATANT.

Or you go to an amusement park
& there's a tunnel of love
& pictures of straights
painted on the front
& grinning couples
coming in and out.
BUT GAYS SHOULDN'T BE BLATANT.

Fact is, blatant heterosexuals
are all over the place.
Supermarkets, movies, on your job,
in church, in books, on television
every day and night, every place —
even in gay bars.
& they want gay men & women
to go hide in the closets —

So to you straight folks
i say — Sure, i'll go
if you go too,
but i'm polite —
so — after you.

My Lady Ain't No Lady

my lady ain't no lady

she doesn't flow into a room —
she enters & her presence is felt.
she doesn't sit small —
she takes all her space.
she doesn't partake of meals —
she eats — replenishes herself.

my lady ain't no lady —

she has been known
        to speak in loud voice,
        to pick her nose,
        stumble on a sidewalk,
        swear at her cats,
        swear at me,
        scream obscenities at men,
        paint rooms,
        repair houses,
        tote garbage,
        play basketball,
        & numerous other
        un lady like things.

my lady is definitely no lady
which is fine with me,

cause i ain't no gentleman.

Non-monogamy Is A Pain In The Butt

I have a lover
who has a lover
who has a lover
now, ain't that hot.

So one day
i say, hey
why don't you stay?
she said, tonight
i'd rather not.

My lover and me
decided to be
two, not four or three
surely you see,
but thanks a lot.

I have a lover
who has a lover
who has a lover
now that's a dumb spot.

But it's okay
tomorrow we'll play
be loving and gay
maybe stroll by the bay
& take pictures of yachts

So don't laugh, he hee
at my lovers and me
what a strange place to be
For you can't foresee
what's to be your lot.

Maybe one day
you will say
with hair turning gray
and heart heavy as clay
laying alone on a cot.

I have a lover
who has a lover
who has a lover
now ain't that hot.

LOVE POEMS

love

& friendship

are words of

people

telling

people

trust is
a word
for
bankers

me

& you

&

You

are

words

for

us.

Let me come to you naked
come without my masks
come dark
    and lay beside you

Let me come to you old
come as a dying snail
come weak
    and lay beside you

Let me come to you angry
come shaking with hate
come callused
    and lay beside you

even more

Let me come to you strong
come sure and free
come powerful

and lay with you

I have a solitary lover
  she digs it
    moves with it
        moves
            alone well
        moves alone
            well
  i have a solitary
        lover
  she digs it
  she digs moving
    digs
        moving
        alone
& when i barge
    into her world
        she
            in spite of herself
        graciously
                comes
        with me
                calms with me
            solitary

I Kumquat You

Some one said

to say,

I love you -

is corny.

A Small Contradiction

It is politically incorrect
to demand monogamous
relationships -

It's emotionally insecure
to seek
ownership of
another's soul -
or body &
damaging to one's psyche
to restrict the giving and
taking of love.

Me, i am
totally opposed to
monogamous relationships
unless
i'm
in love.

i wish that i could hate you
when you brush against me in sleep
your breath slapping life in my innards
& i feel my body go soft in wanting you
i wish right then that i could hate you

i wish that i could hate you
when i sit not able to see you
cursing the something that came up
& know i will still come when you call -
i wish right then that i could hate you

i wish that i could hate you
when i hear you on the phone
planning time away from me
& wish it was me that you're talking to
i wish right then that i could hate you

I wish for enough anger to hate you
- My love for you keeps getting in my way.

Bitch!
i want to scream
I hate you
Fuck you for this pain
You used my guts
& now you stand here
Write my pain off
an unworkable experience
Bitch!
i want to scream -
& the words -
- unreal
from my mouth
i love you -
i hope you'll be happy.

Sitting here,
        listening to you
make music.
        i realized
the many years
        we
                have known each other
        is
one month.

        so instead
                of running upstairs
& sticking my tongue
        in your ear
                i'll give you
                        this.

Both gestures
        mean
                the same.

Woman, i love you.

If it were possible
to place you in my brain,
to let you roam
around in and out
my thought waves —
you would never
have to ask —
why do you love me?

This morning as you slept,
i wanted to kiss you awake —
say "i love you" til your brain
smiled and nodded, "yes"
this woman does love me.

Each day the list grows —
filled with the things that are you
things that make my heart jump —
Yet, words would sound strange;
become corny in utterance.

Now, each morning when i wake
i don't look out my window
to see if the sun is shining —
i turn to you — instead.

I HAVE
(for Laura K. Brown)

i have known
many women
& the you of you
puzzles me.

it is not beauty
i have known
beautiful women.

it is not brains
i have known
intelligent women.

it is not goodness
i have known
good women.

it is not selflessness
i have known
giving women.

Yet, you touch me
in new,
different
ways

i become sand
on a beach
washed anew with
each wave of you.

with each touch of you
i am fresh bread
warm and rising

i become a new-born kitten
ready to be licked
& nuzzled into life.

You are my last love
And my first love
You make me a virgin-

& I want to give myself to you

ON JEALOUSY

It's insane
& childish
you say
your feeling —
makes you embarrassed

my body responds to you —
glows with your touch
feels mellow —
safe & protected.
childish,
insane, you say —

no say i —
i worry about
people who don't
care for
or value
their
possessions

As you entered
  my life -
it was so easy
  to accept -
for years
i have
visualized
  you & me
    on beaches
    in stores
    at movies
    in bed

Fantasy is the food
        of poets
what blew my mind-
is when i pinched
myself to wake up-
        & YOU
were still
        here.

Metamorphosis

you take these fingers
        bid them soft —
a velvet touch
        to your loins

you take these arms
        bid them pliant
a warm cocoon
        to shield you

you take this shell
        bid it full
a sensual cup
        to lay with you

you take this voice
        bid it sing
an uncaged bird
        to warble your praise

you take me, love
        a sea skeleton
fill me with you
        & i become
pregnant with love
        give birth
                to revolution

Para Maria Sandra

Pain, like fertilizer
can be used for growth
can be worked
deep inside —
nurtured
turned to blossoms.

i have felt you
pequena gigante
as i move
across the land
of your past

Seen the strength
of your reds & browns
— the subtle power

To ease your pain
to soothe your anger
i would become
the grandmother
would stroke your hair
and lie
es nada, nina
es nada.

i would become
the unknown father
would take you
in my arms

& speak to you
of my pride
sing praise of
our blood.

I would become
the brother
locked in silence —
trapped in manhood
would speak
forever of love
be gentle & touch

To ease your pain
i would become
a chameleon
change to your needs
i would become
tu familia
te amo
pequena gigante
te amo.

gente

it's difficult to explain
a good feeling-
my world has become colorful-
a rainbow of hues
now- a part of my living
    and it feels good.

it feels good
to listen to people
talk about the streets
& know
it's not a *vicarious* experience.

it feels good
to sit and be loose
to talk, without worry,
about the racist in the room.

it feels good
to hear
'we're gonna have a party'
& know it's really
going to be a party.

it feels good
to be able to say
my sisters
and not have
any reservations.

But best of all-
it feels good
to sit in a room
and say
'Have you ever felt like..?'
and somebody has.

GROUP

"the primary lesson learned
by any minority is self-hatred"

I do not know
when my lessons began

I have no memory
    of a teacher,
    or books.

osmosis — perhaps
the lessons slip
into my brain,
my cells — silently

I do have memory of
    childhood chants

if you're white — alright
if you're brown — stick around
if you're Black — get back

I do have memory of teachers

*"you are heathens
why can't you be
like the white kids
you are bad —"*

Bad

& I never thought
to ask the Black teachers
in the all Black schools
How did they know
how white kids were?

Bad

I do have memory
of playground shouts
"your lips are too big"
a memory of my sisters
putting lipstick
on half of their lips
to make them look smaller

Bad

"your hair is nappy"
I do have memory
of "Beauty" parlours
& hot combs and grease

Bad

*"stay out of the sun
it'll make you darker"*
I do have memory
of Black & White
bleaching cream
Nadinola
Bleach & Glow

Bad

"your nose is too big"

I do have memory
of mothers pinching
their babies' noses
to make them smaller
    Bad
    BAD
I do not know
when my lessons
    began
do not know
when my lessons
    were learned,
absorbed into my cells

    now
there are new lessons
    new teachers
each week I go to my group
    see women
        Black women
Beautiful Black Women
& I am in love
    with each of them
& this is important
    in the loving
in the act of loving
    each woman
I have learned a new lesson
I have learned
    to love myself

The Law

In my youth
i was taught
the law is good —
my parents,
my teachers,
    all
told of policemen
to help me find my way —
of courts, to punish
those who would harm me
i was taught
"respect the law"
Now, in my third decade
I have seen the law

the law
comes to homes
& takes the poor
for traffic tickets
the law
takes people to jail
for stealing food
the law
comes in mini-skirts
to see if your home
is bare enough
for welfare
the law
sits in robes
in courtrooms
& takes away

your children
the law
arrests the prostitute
but not her customer
the law
sends a rich woman
to jail on weekends
for murder
sends a porno book seller
to jail for 30 years
the law
tries women who kill
rapists &
frees the rapist
because rape
is a "normal"
reaction
And my mind reels
    contradictions
    contra/
        dictions
& the voices from
my youth declare

the law is *good*
the law is *fair*
the law is *just*
& then I realize
good, fair, just,
are all 4 letter words
& to use 4 letter words
is against the law

WOMANSLAUGHTER

It doesn't hurt as much now —
the thought of you dead
doesn't rip at my innards,
leaves no holes to suck rage.
Now, thoughts of the four
daughters of Buster Cooks,
children, survivors
of Texas Hell, survivors
of soul-searing poverty,
survivors of small town
mentality, survivors,
now three
doesn't hurt as much now.

I
An Act

I used to be fearful
of phone calls in the night —
never in the day.

Death, like the vampire
fears the sun
never in the day —
"Hello Patty"
"Hey big sister
what's happening?
How's the kids?"
"Patty, Jonesy shot Shirley.
She didn't make it."

Hello, Hello Death
Don't you know it's daytime?
The sun is much too bright today
Hello, Hello Death
you made a mistake
came here too soon, again.
Five months, Death
My sisters and I just met
in celebration of you —
We came, the four strong
daughters of Buster Cooks,
and buried him —
We came the four strong
daughters of Buster Cooks,
and took care of his widow.
We came the four strong
daughters of Buster Cooks
and shook hands with his friends.
We came, the four strong
daughters of Buster Cooks,
and picked the right flowers.
We came, the four strong
daughters of Buster Cooks,
walked tall & celebrated you.
We came, his four strong daughters,
and notified insurance companies,
arranged social security payments,
gathered the sum of his life.

"We must be strong for mother."

She was the third daughter of Buster Cooks.
I am the fourth.
And in his death we met.
The four years that separated us — gone.
And we talked.
She would divorce the quiet man.
Go back to school — begin again.
Together we would be strong
& take care of Buster's widow.
The poet returned to the family.
The fourth daughter came home.

Hello, Hello Death
What's this you say to me?
Now there are three.
We came, the three sisters
of Shirley Jones,
& took care of her mother.
We picked the right flowers,
contacted insurance companies,
arranged social security payments,
and cremated her.
We came, the three sisters
of Shirley Jones.
We were not strong.
"It is good, they said,
that Buster is dead.
He would surely kill
the quiet man."

II
Justice

There was a quiet man
He married a quiet wife
Together, they lived
a quiet life.

Not so, not so
her sisters said,
the truth comes out
as she lies dead.
He beat her.
He accused her
of awful things
& he beat her.
One day she left.

"Hello, Hello Police
I am a woman
& I am afraid.
My husband means to kill me."

She went to her sister's house
She, too, was a woman alone.
The quiet man came & beat her.
Both women were afraid.

"Hello, Hello Police
I am a woman
& I am afraid
My husband means to kill me."

The four strong daughters
of Buster Cooks
came to bury him —
the third one carried a gun.
"Why do you have a gun?"
"For protection — just in case."
"Can you shoot it?"
"Yes, I have learned well."

"Hello, Hello Police
I am a woman alone
& I am afraid.
My husband means to kill me."

"Lady, there's nothing we can do
until he tries to hurt you.
Go to the judge & he will decree
that your husband leaves you be."
She found an apartment
with a friend.
She would begin
a new life again.
Interlocutory Divorce Decree in hand;
The end of the quiet man.
He came to her home
& he beat her
Both women were afraid.

"Hello, Hello Police
I am a woman alone
& I am afraid
My ex-husband means to kill me."

"Fear not, lady
He will be sought."
It was *too* late,
when he was caught.
One day a quiet man
shot his quiet wife
three times in the back.
He shot her friend as well.
His wife died.

The three sisters
of Shirley Jones
came to cremate her —
They were not strong.

III
Somebody's Trial

"It is good, they said
that Buster is dead.
He would surely kill
the quiet man."
I was not at the trial.
I was not needed to testify.
She slept with other men, he said.
No, said her friends.
No, said her sisters.
That is a lie.

She was Black.
You are white.
Why were you there?
We were friends, she said.
I was helping her move
the furniture; the divorce court
had given it to her.
Were you alone? they asked.
No two men came with us.
They were gone with a load.
She slept with women, he said.
No, said her sisters.
No, said her friends.
We were only friends;
That is a lie.
You lived with this woman?
Yes, said her friend.
You slept in the same bed?
Yes, said her friend.
Were you lovers?
No, said her friend.
But you slept in the same bed?
Yes, said her friend.

What shall be done with this man?
Is it a murder of the first degree?
No, said the men,
It is a crime of passion.
He was angry.

Is it a murder of second degree?
Yes, said the men,
but we will not call it that.
We must think of his record.
We will call it manslaughter.
The sentence is the same.
What will we do with this man?
His boss, a white man came.
This is a quiet Black man, he said.
He works well for me
The men sent the quiet
Black man to jail.
He went to work in the day.
He went to jail & slept at night.
In one year, he went home.

IV
Woman-slaughter

"It is good, they said,
that Buster is dead.
He would surely kill
the quiet man."

Sister, I do not understand.
I rage & do not understand.
In Texas, he would be freed.
One Black kills another
One less Black for Texas.
But this is not Texas.
This is California.
The city of angels.
Was his crime so slight?

George Jackson served
years for robbery.
Eldridge Cleaver served
years for rape.
I know of a man in Texas
who is serving 40 years
for possession of marijuana.
Was his crime *so* slight?
What was his crime?
He only killed his wife.
But a divorce I say.
Not final, they say;
Her things were his
including her life.
Men cannot rape their wives.
Men cannot kill their wives.
They passion them to death.

The three sisters
of Shirley Jones
came & cremated her.
& they were not strong.
Hear me now —
It is almost three years
& I am again strong.

I have gained many sisters.
And if one is beaten,
or raped, or killed,
I will not come in mourning black.
I will not pick the right flowers.

I will not celebrate her death
& it will matter not
if she's Black or white —
if she loves women or men.
I will come with my many sisters
and decorate the streets
with the innards of those
brothers in womenslaughter.
No more, can I dull my rage
in alcohol & deference
to *men's* courts.
I will come to my sisters,
not dutiful,
I will come strong.

Autumn Morning
  for Shirley

Tree--
    that lives
    & feeds
    & feels
--from the living,
--from the dead,
      you grow.

Tree--
    in time,
i will move
in dawn stillness,
    with you.

"Her children arise up, and call
her blessed....."

proverbs 31:28

when i was a child
i was punished —
i refused to say
yes sir & yes mam.
i was — they said
disrespectful —
should extend
        courtesy —
defer to age.
i believe
        respect
is earned —
does not come
with birth.
now, my mother
is dying
& i wish to say
so much,
to thank her
to say — i love you
to hold her in my arms.
these things
i cannot do/
we have too
many years
of not touching —
of not saying

Instead — i sit
& watch her sleep —
see her breathe —
        labor
cringe at the tubes
in her body/
watch the strength
        seep away
i am afraid of death
fear to touch a cold body
yet, i know
in the final viewing,
i will lean over my mother
& whisper in her ear —
yes mam, mama, yes mam.

there is a woman in this town

she goes to different bars
sits in the remotest place
watches the other people
drinks til 2 & goes home - alone

some say she is lonely
some say she is an agent
none of us speak to her

Is she our sister?

there is a woman in this town
she lives with her husband
she raises her children
she says she is happy
& is not a women's libber

some say she is mis-guided
some say she is an enemy
none of us know her

Is she our sister?

there is a woman in this town

she carries a lot of weight
her flesh triples on her frame
she comes to all the dances
dances a lot; goes home - alone

some say she's a lot of fun
some say she is too fat
none of us have loved her

Is she our sister?

there is a woman in this town

she owns her own business
she goes to work in the day
she goes home at night
she does not come to the dances

some say she is a capitalist
some say she has no consciousness
none of us trust her

Is she our sister?

there is a woman in this town

she comes to all the parties
wears the latest men's fashions
calls the women mama
& invites them to her home

some say she's into roles
some say she hates herself
none of us go out with her

Is she our sister?

there is a woman in this town

she was locked up
she comes to many meetings
she volunteers for everything
she crys when she gets upset

some say she makes them nervous
some say she's too pushy
none of us invite her home

Is she our sister?

there is a woman in this town

she fills her veins with dope
goes from house to house to sleep
borrows money wherever she can
she pays it back if she must

some say she is a thief
some say she drains their energy
none of us have trusted her

Is she our sister?

once upon a time, there was a dream
a dream of women. a dream of women
coming together and turning the world
around. turning the world around and making it over
a dream of women, all women being sisters.
a dream of caring; a dream of protection, a dream
of peace.

once upon a time, there was a dream
a dream of women. for the women who rejected the
dream; there had only been a reassurance. for the
women who believed the dream - there is dying, women,
sisters dying
     once upon a time there was a dream, a dream of women
turning the world all over and it still lives-
it lives for those who would be sisters

it lives for those who need a sister
it lives for those who once upon a time had a dream.

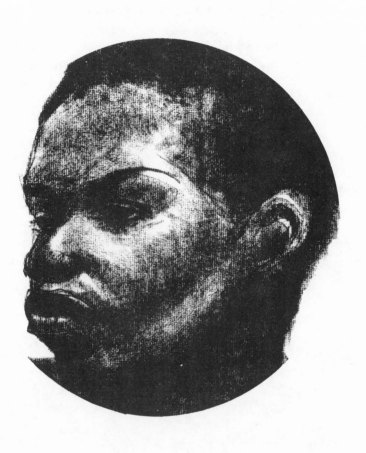

Other titles from Firebrand Books include:

The Big Mama Stories by Shay Youngblood/$8.95

A Burst Of Light, Essays by Audre Lorde/$7.95

Crime Against Nature, Poetry by Minnie Bruce Pratt/$8.95

Diamonds Are A Dyke's Best Friend by Yvonne Zipter/$9.95

Dykes To Watch Out For, Cartoons by Alison Bechdel/$6.95

Eye Of A Hurricane, Stories by Ruthann Robson / $8.95

The Fires Of Bride, A Novel by Ellen Galford/$8.95

A Gathering Of Spirit, A Collection by North American Indian Women
edited by Beth Brant *(Degonwadonti)/$9.95*

Getting Home Alive by Aurora Levins Morales and Rosario Morales
/$8.95

Good Enough To Eat, A Novel by Lesléa Newman/$8.95

Humid Pitch, Narrative Poetry by Cheryl Clarke/$8.95

Jonestown & Other Madness, Poetry by Pat Parker/$7.95

The Land Of Look Behind, Prose and Poetry by Michelle Cliff/$6.95

A Letter To Harvey Milk, Short Stories by Lesléa Newman/$8.95

Letting In The Night, A Novel by Joan Lindau/$8.95

Living As A Lesbian, Poetry by Cheryl Clarke/$7.95

Making It, A Woman's Guide to Sex in the Age of AIDS by Cindy
Patton and Janis Kelly/$3.95

Metamorphosis, Reflections On Recovery, by Judith McDaniel/$7.95

Mohawk Trail by Beth Brant *(Degonwadonti)*/$6.95

Moll Cutpurse, A Novel by Ellen Galford/$7.95

More Dykes To Watch Out For, Cartoons by Alison Bechdel/$7.95

The Monarchs Are Flying, A Novel by Marion Foster/$8.95

My Mama's Dead Squirrel, Lesbian Essays on Southern Culture by
Mab Segrest/$8.95

The Other Sappho, A Novel by Ellen Frye/$8.95

Politics Of The Heart, A Lesbian Parenting Anthology edited by Sandra
Pollack and Jeanne Vaughn/$11.95

Presenting. . .Sister NoBlues by Hattie Gossett/$8.95

A Restricted Country by Joan Nestle/$8.95

(continued)

Sanctuary, A Journey by Judith McDaniel/$7.95

Sans Souci, And Other Stories by Dionne Brand/$8.95

Shoulders, A Novel by Georgia Cotrell/$8.95

The Sun Is Not Merciful, Short Stories by Anna Lee Walters/$7.95

Tender Warriors, A Novel by Rachel Guido deVries/$7.95

This Is About Incest by Margaret Randall/$7.95

The Threshing Floor, Short Stories by Barbara Burford/$7.95

Trash, Stories by Dorothy Allison/$8.95

The Women Who Hate Me, Poetry by Dorothy Allison/$5.95

Words To The Wise, A Writer's Guide to Feminist and Lesbian Periodicals & Publishers by Andrea Fleck Clardy/$3.95

Yours In Struggle, Three Feminist Perspectives on Anti-Semitism and Racism by Elly Bulkin, Minnie Bruce Pratt, and Barbara Smith /$8.95

You can buy Firebrand titles at your bookstore, or order them directly from the publisher (141 The Commons, Ithaca, New York 14850, 607-272-0000).

Please include $1.75 shipping for the first book and $.50 for each additional book.

A free catalog is available on request.